Ganesh.

Removing the Obstacles

James H. Bae

MANDALA

San Rafael, California

MANDALA
PUBLISHING

www.MandalaEarth.com

Text © 2003 James Bae

ISBN: 978-1-60109-029-4

Printed in China by Insight Editions

10 9 8 7 6 5

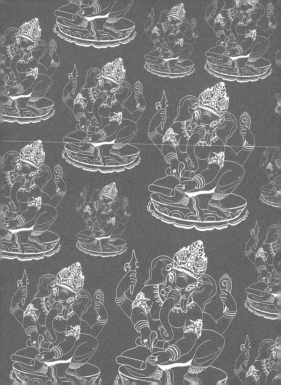

Ganesh.

Removing the Obstacles

Contents

Chapter One

Obstacles

The God of Beginnings

Among his many titles, Ganesh is called the God of Beginnings, for it is at the beginning of a journey, venture or life change—however great or small—that his guidance and protection is sought.

As spiritual beings on a human journey, we share a desire for a

इन्द्र शर्मा

common goal. We seek to be fulfilled. We seek to be enlightened. And, while we are fellow seekers, each one of us follows a unique path. We each arrive at fulfillment by different means and under vastly different conditions. In honoring our uniqueness and the path that is ours alone to take, we find solace.

For countless ages, individuals have sought to answer the enduring question of how to achieve lasting happiness. It is our very nature to desire happiness, the possibility of which is locked within the prison of our human design, chained to the everyday functions of our body, mind and heart. Our purpose, then, is to

explore how this potential for happiness is confined in order to know how it can be freed.

Underlying our existence is a deep intelligence that communicates itself through the dialogue of the "ordinary" events that shape our lives. From this perspective, nothing is accidental, and our notion of the triviality of daily experience is transcended. Traditional wisdom teaches us that when we participate in this dialogue, we will not only be fulfilled and enjoy the sense of well-being that comes with such fulfillment, but we will contribute to the well-being of others as well. This is so because following one's true path begins with the realization that one's whole being is deeply connected to all of life. ◾

Ganesh in Mythology

Symbolism abounds in the sacred mythology of our wisdom traditions. This lore acts as a guide in which to navigate the symbols, or signals, which appear in our everyday lives. The paradox we live with, of course, is that while the fundamental lessons from which we seek to learn present themselves as tangible life situations, we often fail to recognize or engage them in truly instructional ways because of our own habits and misconceptions. The understanding we desire is within us, but we must first learn to see. This book, while diminutive in size, offers practical and meaningful interpretations of folk narratives and sacred texts about the larger-than-life elephant-headed god, Ganesh.

Ganesh appears in many forms, signifying the diversity of human destiny. In South Indian traditions, he is unmarried and fully devoted to his mother, Parvati. In the North, Ganesh is a householder with two consorts, Siddhi and Buddhi, known as Achievement and Wisdom, respectively. As Bala Ganesh, the divine child, he is curious and full of folly. He is playful and loving, though he understands deeply the predicament of others. The *modhak*, or sweet confection, he accepts from his beloved devotees is representative not only of his innocence but of the pearls of his wisdom. As the dancing god, Ganesh balances out the severity of every step we take, inspiring realization of the divine behind all of life's circumstances and the joy of living life in concert with the whole. In other forms, Ganesh embodies wisdom and judgment. He is the force of change. In still others, he is the overseer of karma.

Ganesh reigns over both the divine and the demonic and everywhere in between. His powers affect both gods and demons alike, as well as each of us. A paragon of "this-worldliness" and "other-worldliness," Ganesh moves easily and enigmatically between many worlds. Not only is he emblematic of a truth that is all-encompassing, he honors our humanity—our personal hopes, ideals and aspirations—as well as our spirituality. Ganesh teaches us what it is to be truly human. He shows us that the experience of living demands a dynamic search for truth, a daring move from our familiar, and sometimes dangerous, habits and perceptions to a more spontaneous and sincere path—our path to the Divine. ■

Remover of Obstacles

*F*or *Hindus, as well* as many Jains and Buddhists, Ganesh is known as Vighneshvar, the Remover of Obstacles. Hindu devotees worship him for protection during journeys, for the successful performance of their duties, for auspicious benedictions in business matters, as well as for many other basic concerns—for all obstacles

they will no doubt face along the way. Appealing to Ganesh assures that the road will be smooth. Ganesh offers gifts of health and prosperity, connecting one with creation's abundance. He inspires us to understand the deep connection between our worldly experience and that which is spiritual.

Ganesh not only has the power to remove obstacles, but also to put them there in the first place so that we might learn a much-needed lesson or two. What may initially appear as an obstacle can ultimately be seen as a source of strength and a tool for self-exploration and understanding. Ganesh confronts us through the mask of our challenging life circumstances so that we may move about conscientiously and with honest intentions.

In our daily lives, we work to balance all of the elements that are important to us: personal time, work, creativity, family, relationships and spiritual practice. These basic priorities afford us the opportunity to find joy and meaning, while at the same time, meet our practical needs. But it is not easy to establish balance; as we are all well aware, not everything goes as planned.

Oftentimes obstacles challenge us, and it takes perseverance and clarity to meet our needs. But success is not simply about achieving our endeavors, or the end result of

our actions. We need to be able to recognize the unexpected openings, or opportunities, that obstacles offer. One believes that there is only destiny, and another, that magic and infinite possibility underlie every living situation. One belief without the other is incomplete—in order to overcome our personal obstacles we need to recognize that both possibilities exist, and that life is ultimately full of grace. ■

The Lord of Thresholds

Ganesh is also known as the Lord of Thresholds. In India, statues of Ganesh are placed at the inner gates of many temples symbolizing his role as a keeper of sacred spaces. Here, pilgrims and passersby pay homage and seek his blessings. It is this symbolic presence at the entrance of our most holy places that makes Ganesh such a vital figure in our lives. Stationed at the threshold of sacredness and awareness, mediating between the possibility of the profound and our often habitual, mundane perception of the world, Ganesh is the guiding force behind this very moment of experience—where our human desire meets possibility.

In another sense, Ganesh stands at the threshold of old and new, the sacred and the profane, the wisdom of obsolete religious and social practices and the complex modern age we live in. He is a bridge connecting a truthful way of living, or dharma, from the distant past to the present. ■

The Bridge of Dharma

Dharma addresses our sense of separation from the Absolute, the search for individual fulfillment and collective well-being and the notion of adapting our inherited wisdom and values into the present. Dharma is the very essence of life. It connects all beings and things together in harmony.

In direct contrast with the notion of dharma is our infatuation with individual experience, singular fulfillment and our desire for pleasure. The root cause of suffering and despair is narcissism, our sense of separateness. It is not our desire for pleasure that causes dissatisfaction, it is the disconnection with the spiritual that results when we place so much of our potential for happiness into the pursuit of material pleasure. Pleasure is only misery masked in the garb of temporary fulfillment.

We are fulfilled when we discover the reason for our creation and live truthfully. But our happiness depends not solely on being personally fulfilled,

but on contributing to the fulfillment of others. The gift of our uniqueness is not a gift for us alone: it is given so that we may share it with our family, our community and with God.

Dharma is a universal principle that engages us through our precious experiences so that we progress. Life reveals dharmic insights into how best to live truthfully and with integrity. The deeper we explore this concept, the closer we are to freeing ourselves from the constraints of personal desire. ■

Blessings from Ganesh

T*wo objects often associated* with Ganesh are his noose and his goad. As symbols these objects represent a life that is both individually nourishing and universally sustaining, or balanced.

The noose is a fear-inducing icon, one that is meant to deter individuals from performing acts that are harmful to themselves or others. When we try to assert ourselves in detrimental ways, life seems to pull the reins. Even when we think we have positive intentions, we might not necessarily see the whole picture. Ganesh's noose reminds us that we need to slow down and examine our intentions, to ensure that they are honest. Otherwise, we might find ourselves in uncomfortable, even threatening positions.

Similarly, Ganesh's goad encourages us in dharmic ways. The sharp goad represents the narrow and often challenging obstacle-strewn path one must walk. It is also said to represent protection. Ganesh protects us and opens doors in our lives so that we can proceed with confidence. When nothing stands in the way of our efforts, or when we arrive safely, we can perceive it as a blessing from Ganesh. ∎

Chapter Two

Self-Understanding

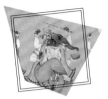

The Play of the Divine

Once, Ganesh was riding on his vehicle, the mouse, and ravenously consuming handfuls of his dessert of choice, *modhak*—a sweet confection made of milk, flour and sugar. Suddenly, a snake crossed their path. Naturally the mouse shrieked and reared back out of fear, and the great Ganesh fell onto the ground, belly first. Upon

impact, his rotund belly exploded and all of the sweets he had eaten poured out in every direction. Upset, Ganesh grabbed the snake and tied his belly back together with it. Meanwhile, up above, the moon laughed at the whole

event. So, Ganesh pulled out one of his tusks and threw it at the moon, and darkness fell upon the earth. Later the moon was restored, but because of the damage wrought by Ganesh's tusk, it was never whole again. That is why the moon appears to wax and wane.

Using iconography and imagery associated with Ganesh, this myth explains the phenomenon of the lunar cycle. In traditional contexts, narratives that surround the gods, such as this one, are called *lila*, or "the play of the divine." *Lila* narratives portray the folly of the gods in contrast to the actual power, freedom and grace the gods more often exhibit. From outside of tradition, the myths that surround different deities are but stories fabricated to communicate universal themes. Within the tradition, differing views can only be reconciled by devotion and personal experience of the divinity of the deity; otherwise details remain a mere mystery.

Ganesh's anger in this telling scenario shows just how caught up in our emotions we can get, and, in turn, how defensive we can act, especially when we find ourselves at the center of criticism or ridicule. Such a response reveals how strongly we are attached to our self-image and what we will do to restore and maintain it at all costs. Attachment to our emotions can make us cling to the outer appearance of

things and take us away from the truth.

Beyond emotion, there is reason. Reason allows us to take inventory of our personal reality. With reason we understand our emotions—the emotions that detract from our full involvement in life.

But reason can become a problem when we try to rationalize our negative behavior or interpret it in self-centered ways. The overly rational person will evade the truth of the matter by creating a pretty myth, an elaborate self-image, wherein trials become melodramas and trivialities evolve into spectacles that others are forced to admire. Reason and intellect should be tools for honesty and intro-

spection rather than for dressing up our circumstances.

Our emotional and rational selves are deeply connected with our human instincts. Each governs basic functions of human experience. A functional harmony is needed between the two. We lose something of our humanity when we do not address each part of our self. The road to fulfillment requires balance. The play between emotion, reason, and instinct connects us to the outside world, and the more we integrate them, the more we gain. These elements of human personality are but reflections of our soul's inherent nature, which, in an integrated and evolved state, express universal values of wisdom, compassion, truthfulness and loving. The human personality must be fine-tuned and integrated into the work of the soul. The approaches and attitudes to such work are reflected in the interpretations of Ganesh mythologies, which illustrate how to purposefully integrate our feeling, thinking and instinct into our lives.

Each of our lives has a unique design. Each of us has a unique purpose in this lifetime. The lessons we need to learn are deeply embedded within us and demand an unfolding or widening of our sense of self. But that sense is subtle and complex. Uncovering our deepest self from the layers of self-image is an arduous task. Fulfillment can only occur when we are alive to our highest potential, to a sense of self beyond our many roles and sides. This is the part of us that survives all the struggles and predicaments that we face. It has taken us through the gateway of birth and remains beyond the frontier of death. This self is joyous and radiant. It never wrestles with dissatisfaction and is the deepest basis of our personhood or presence. Knowing this self is to be enlightened.

We begin to sense this deepest self as the very thread of continuity that underlies our daily experience. What changes is merely our external identity and behavior, both of which are influenced by our humanity. The balance of emotion, reason and instinct that we maintain in our personal lives affects our self-understanding. The following narrative reveals much about how we function in both freedom and bondage, and about the play of feeling, rationality and passion. ∎

The Divine Child

According to Hindu lore, Ganesh is the son of Parvati, the goddess of creation and wife of Lord Shiva, the god of destruction. The story of Ganesh's birth and how he came to have the head of an elephant reveals, quite literally, the necessity of keeping an attitude of open-mindedness in the face of obstacles.

In the story, Parvati was bathing in her private sanctuary. Shiva had ventured off to perform austerities. Feeling lonely and longing for a child, Parvati yearned for the company and affection of a son. Mimicking the manner in which the world was created, she shaped the form of a beautiful boy from an earthen mixture and brought him to life. Parvati loved the child and was no longer alone. He guarded the entrance of her private bath to ward off any intruders as she continued bathing in privacy.

When Shiva returned home, he found a stranger at Parvati's door. Out of obedience to his mother's orders the child refused the mighty god entrance into her bathing area. Vexed, Shiva unleashed his wild fury and the boy's head fell from his body.

Upon discovering what had happened to her beloved child, Parvati grieved and would not leave her sanctuary until Shiva replaced the head of her beautiful boy. Shiva's attendants went out in search of the first being they saw, to be sacrificed so that Shiva could keep his promise. The first being they found was an elephant. Soon the child was brought back to life with that elephant's head. He became known as Gajanana, or Ganesh, the "Elephant-headed One."

Just as there are many ways to interpret mythology, there are infinite ways to perceive any given situation. A single event can cause a spectrum of feelings in as many people. We must learn to examine just how settled we are in the way we view things. Without a desire to see more deeply, we remain closed to the depth of life's events and live only on the surface, in the limited sphere of our projections.

Ganesh's beginnings also teach us that spiritual transformation requires a profound turn within. His decapitation symbolizes a freedom from ego, a retreat into a space of unknowing. In our lives, we are vulnerable to challenging experiences just as Parvati's child was vulnerable to Shiva's wrath. Such experiences as illness, life

changes and the loss of loved ones,
allow us to see that our only way out
is to move within and to meet tragedy
and uncertainty with inner-stability.
This inward focus allows us to see
that our many experiences unite with
the will of God. ■

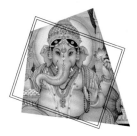

Boundaries

In the story of Ganesh's mystical birth, he is stationed as a keeper at the door of his mother's sanctuary. His duty is to protect her from intruders. As the Lord of Thresholds, Ganesh reminds us about the importance of guarding our space and setting boundaries.

Boundaries are not necessarily limitations. They can be practical guidelines we uphold for functionality. We set boundaries to assure that we give ourselves the space we need to develop

our inner-lives and to live with integrity. Throughout our lives, from childhood to adulthood to old age, we constantly reshape the boundaries of our identity. As our lives change and we develop as individuals, old boundaries dissolve and new ones form. Life circumstances keep changing and hopefully we keep evolving. Boundaries lose their efficacy when we regard them as absolutes. At some point, we let go of boundaries. We learn to define ourselves and our beliefs beyond the bounds of dogmas and social norms. In the face of truth, our boundaries collapse. Ganesh reveals to us that eventually we have to let down our guard and remain sensitive to the messages at hand. ■

Bowing to Truth

Ganesh is also known as Ekadanta because he appears with one tusk. Some scriptures say Ganesh lost his tusk in battle with a great warrior sage named Parashuram. According to ancient Vedic record, Parashuram, regarded as an avatar of Vishnu, single-handedly defeated a ruling warrior class and re-established religion according to true Vedic principles, as it had become corrupted over time. In his battle with Ganesh, Parashuram represents "the face of truth" and Ganesh represents the wisdom of "bowing to truth."

Parashuram wished to pay homage to Shiva at his holy abode of Kailash. There at the entrance he met Ganesh, who was positioned so that no one would disturb his father. Parashuram was not inclined to listen to this mere child and proceeded eagerly to see Shiva. Ganesh stood his ground and would not allow the great sage to enter.

A fierce battle ensued between the two. Finally, Parashuram wielded his famed axe and hurled it at his opponent. When Ganesh saw this amazing weapon, he recognized it as a sign from Shiva—the weapon was originally Shiva's own—and bowed to it, in the direction of grace. The axe struck Ganesh breaking his tusk, and he allowed Parashuram to enter.

When we are dedicated to truth and living with integrity, sometimes we know to "bow" in circumstances others might see as our time of gain. We bow because in this moment we sense our highest purpose, and we understand that the real gain is, and can only be, an internal one.

Outwardly, we may at times step away or retreat from relative success. Some scriptures say that Ganesh was beginning to get the upper hand in his battle with Parashuram. In this encounter, Ganesh teaches us to seek the essence in any situation. In our lives, this sense of choosing to follow what is essential may take the form of not accepting a job offer which might bring monetary gain, but in the long run would detract time from a rewarding personal relationship or spiritual practice. It could also mean not needing to be "right" in an argument when one actually is, or not accepting undue praise.

Bowing to truth also means recognizing that truth is ever-present and appears in unlimited forms in order to engage and teach us. The story of Ganesh bowing to his opponent inspires the act of "seeing" or recognizing the hand of God in the ordinary events of our daily lives. Ganesh's single tusk signifies this realization, that there is an essential unity or connectedness in all things. Revelation is not bound only to sacred words scripted on palm leaves, but can be seen in and as the world in every moment. We can engage in life in this way when we have established contentment and acceptance in our hearts. ■

Chapter Three

Life Approaches

The Way of Wisdom

There is no adequate map of the terrain of personal growth, but there are universal roads that individuals have traveled to achieve happiness. The story of Ganesh and Skanda weaves together some basic themes of aspiration and journey.

Once there was a friendly dispute between Ganesh and Skanda over who should be considered senior among the two divine siblings. The matter was to be resolved in a race. Whoever could circle the universe and return first would receive the position. Skanda, in his youthful prowess, quickly boarded his peacock mount and raced off, leaving Ganesh in his wake.

Ganesh was not deterred, although his own companion, the mouse, was no challenge to the mount of his brother. Without speaking, he folded his hands in prayer. Then he slowly and reverently circumambulated his parents, Shiva and Parvati, and bowed his head when he was done. When asked about the meaning of his action, Ganesh stated that one's parents are the center

of the universe and that by circumam-
bulating them, he had made a full pas-
sage. Pleased by his devotion, Shiva
and Parvati declared him the senior.

This narrative illustrates the power
of devotion and dedication in overcoming challenges in our lives. From a
spiritual perspective, there are essen-
tially two paths to development: the way

of wisdom and the way of love or devotion.

The way of wisdom involves discernment and strict renunciation. Discernment means deciphering between truth and falsehood and applying that realization according to time and circumstance. The way of love or devotion entails self-surrender to God. It is a path of humility, service and joy.

Either way is a genuine path to overcoming obstacles and articulates the approaches to achieving lasting fulfillment—that of effort and of grace. In either case, the spiritual path requires skill, sensitivity and discretion in action. Our actions and intentions bring us either limitation or freedom depending on how we choose to act.

Like the young and robust Skanda, we may recognize a certain tendency in ourselves to get caught up in the lure of outward success. Skanda reveals the need to be able to actualize our goals with dedication and perseverance. We need to bridge personal conviction with practical and pragmatic service.

The treasure of our true self is beyond the grasp of any narcissistic concern. Ganesh signals us to be clear and responsive to our heart's call and to honor the duties we are granted. ■

The Spirit of the Journey

The demands of everyday life are endless. Obligations and desires can preoccupy us and keep us from fully living. But then, the life we live can be dynamic and creative if we don't let obstacles block the flow of our conscious existence, hiding the truth in daily life.

Our work in life involves first developing a healthy sense of personhood and then transcending and integrating it. Along the way, traumas or conflicts occur that condition us and challenge our growth. Much of our time is spent just maintaining our emotional lives and physical conditions. To move ahead, we often have to clear the trail as we go. Progress and development do not occur without change in our motivations and actions.

One of many symbols that adorn the images of Ganesh is the *svastika*, which represents the dynamic unity of all things with their source. Each spoke or branch of the *svastika* has vertical and horizontal lines, symbolizing our individual paths to fulfillment that are crooked like the movement of a snake or a winding trail through the forest. Our commitment to truth must be one of radical honesty and, consequently, flexibility.

Each bend of our life's course embodies a natural harmony—one that is both guided and created by each step we take. At every juncture, at every moment, the situations we face fit the design of our life course. They are orchestrated to help us develop our human potential and, if we recognize their inherent value, they facilitate positive movements in our personal progression. The winding paths that we traverse involve both a degree of personal determination to find fulfillment, and a sense of abandon or willingness to let our lives unfold as they may. In any of these movements, we must remain loyal to our heart. Otherwise, we act not out of love and care but out of denial, repression or rationalization of unprogressive attitudes. The measure of progress is to leave behind the old and embrace new growth and development.

Over and again we come to crossroads in our lives—critical junctions where we are forced to take leaps of faith to regain what is essential. As Guardian of Thresholds, Ganesh teaches us that these junctures are the times to jump, to make decisions and embrace any changes that are necessary to move forward. The choices we make at these moments largely determine the course of our personal development and the circumstances that lie ahead of us.

Every stage of our lives comes to a natural end. Our work and our relationships, which largely define our sense of identity, are pervaded with a sense of finality. At some point, an inner-shift occurs when all of these chapters of our lives hold no meaning for us and we are called to address higher pursuits. ■

Life in the Real

The distinction between worldly and spiritual life is nebulous—the spiritual and the material are inextricably bound. The life we live either reflects this essential harmony or is wrought with seeming contradictions and challenges that call for this realization. Ganesh reconnects us with the present moment of experience wherein we realize its connection to the Divine. Our life pathway is one of innocence, of listening and of accepting the circumstances dealt to us. Personal freedom is met through challenging ordeals, the purpose of which is to skillfully liberate us from the grips of ego that bind us. Life is sacred. Our deeds should embrace this noblest of truths.

Ganesh—in all his forms—impresses upon us the idea of an honest and complete human life. He is at the heart of an evolving mythology, whose interpretation and inspiration yield instruction for living a practical life. Embodied within this wisdom is a spiritual impetus that compels us to live the truth sought in all ages by all people of free will and heart.

Aware of the passions that uphold the human spirit and the truth that brings relevance and harmony, Ganesh offers a beginning, a path of faith—a positive and intentional approach to living. It is a path that moves in spontaneity: beyond form and formlessness, beyond personality and impersonality, and beyond dogma and disobedience. It is neither the ascetic path, nor that of the aesthete. It is an inner-following and an honest joyfulness, an undefined way of the heart flowing from the depth of Being. ■